KV-194-863

AN EXAMINATION GUIDE for NURSERY NURSES

Jean Brain, Cert. Ed.
Molly D. Martin, S.R.N., H.V. Cert.

HULTON EDUCATIONAL

Acknowledgements

The authors wish to thank *Nursery World* for making available material which was first published in that magazine.

By the same authors:

CHILD CARE AND HEALTH
for Nursery Nurses

Published by Hulton Educational

First published in Great Britain 1985
by Hulton Educational Publications Ltd
Old Station Drive, Leckhampton,
Cheltenham GL53 0DN

Reprinted with amendments 1986
Reprinted 1988

© *Jean Brain and Molly D. Martin* 1985

All rights reserved. No part of this publication may be reproduced, stored in a retrieval system, or transmitted in any form or by any means, electronic, mechanical, photocopying, recording or otherwise, without the prior written consent of Hulton Educational Publications Ltd

ISBN 0 7175 1366 1

Phototypeset in 10/11pt Linotron Palatino
by Input Typesetting Ltd, London
Printed in Great Britain by Ebenezer Baylis and Son,
Worcester

CONTENTS

	Page
Preparation for your Examination	5
Example 1 of a Multiple Choice Paper	9
Example 1 of an Essay Paper	22
Section A	23
Section B	26
Section C	29
Section D	31
Example 2 of a Multiple Choice Paper	35
Example 2 of an Essay Paper	49
Section A	50
Section B	53
Section C	57
Section D	59
Answers to Multiple Choice Paper 1	62
Answers to Multiple Choice Paper 2	63

PREPARATION FOR YOUR EXAMINATION

If you have done your best, both at your practical training establishments and college throughout your period of training, you should not be feeling panic-stricken now at the prospect of the coming NNEB examinations, nor desperately trying to make up for lost time in the few remaining weeks.

Most students, however, are helped by revision. People differ a good deal in the approaches to revision they find most helpful. By this stage, you probably know what works best for you, but remember, merely temporarily being reminded of subject matter by reading it through does not test your knowledge of it, or your ability to retain it.

It is tempting, particularly if the weather is good, to lie on the lawn with a book open in front of you, at the same time cultivating a tan, and really be no better prepared for your exam at the end of many such hours spent in this way.

It is helpful to draw up a plan of topics for revision. Underline the ones you feel most shaky in, then work systematically through the list, setting yourself so many topics a day, having calculated the rate at which you need to work in order to get through the list in the time available.

Decide on, and keep to, say two hours a day. As you read up each subject, make a brief list of headings as a reminder, e.g., spread of infection: hands, flies, droplets, etc. This is good practice for making a plan when you are actually sitting your examination. Some people find it helpful to write these plans on postcards and carry them around as reminders and aids to revision, but NOT, of course, into the examination room!

After studying your books, notes and other material, strong-mindedly close all books and files, set yourself a likely question on the subject and answer it on paper in *paragraph heading* form only. Later cross-check to see how much you have forgotten.

Equally valuable, and probably more fun, can be getting a parent, brother, sister or friend to 'test' you on selected topics, although it is obviously better if that person is not a complete stranger to the subject.

Although you cannot really predict questions that are likely to come up, there is very often a topical question, so pay attention to aspects of child care which have been in the news this year, possibly allied to social problems or trends, or newly-developing provision for the under-fives.

If you are able to study exam papers for the last year or two (remembering that there are two exams a year), you may decide that certain topics from your syllabus have been neglected and are therefore more likely to appear this time. On the other hand, certain topics are great favourites and crop up frequently in one form or another.

Do not burn the midnight oil for the last few days. You will reach saturation point, and only work yourself into a low physical and mental state. You need the usual sensible pattern of rest, sleep, exercise, proper diet and pleasant social contacts.

Try to retain your sense of proportion and sense of humour throughout. Snapping at the family will only make everyone else edgy, and will not create a relaxed, supportive atmosphere from which you should go forth quietly confident. Try to get some fresh air the morning of the exam, and if you feel trembly or faint, take long, deep breaths; it will have a calming and mentally exhilarating effect.

THE EXAM ITSELF

1. Before you go into the examination

Make sure you have everything you need, e.g., pen and a spare, HB pencil, rubber, ruler, tissues, cough sweets, mascot and anything else you may want with you. Check your watch.

2. Make yourself familiar beforehand with the construction and layout of the examination paper

The first one will consist of 80 multiple-choice questions to be completed in one and three-quarter hours; the second, four essays to be written in three hours.

3. Always read carefully through the instructions before you begin

By doing this you will know exactly what is expected of you, and avoid losing marks unnecessarily.

4. The Multiple-Choice Examination

(a) The questions come in booklet form, and you will also have a separate page in the form of a *grid*, for the correct answers to be marked in (see page 62). You are *not* allowed to make marks on the question booklet, because this will be returned to the Board.

(b) Some students like to cover up the possible answers, and think out what the answer should be, afterwards uncovering the possibilities and settling for the one nearest their own version. Other students like to eliminate certain possibilities which are clearly wrong, then sort out the remaining answers and select the correct one.

(c) Questions setting out a situation, and seeking the best way of dealing with it, often cause difficulty. It is worth remembering that they are usually based on good understanding of 'normal' child development. They are *always* based on good child care practice, as taught at college and promoted by text books. The 'short cuts', and things sometimes said and done in moments of exasperation when dealing with children, day to day, are not what the examiners are requiring.

(d) Once you have made your choice in each case, it is usually good policy to stick to it. You may well find you have a long time left over after completing the paper. By all means read through the questions and check your answers again. But do not be tempted to go over and over choices made, wondering whether there might be hidden 'catches', or more implied than you realised at first.

(e) Do, however, attempt an answer for every question. There is a one in four chance that a mere guess may be right.

5. The Essay Paper

(a) This may make you feel in a panic at first glance. If so, take a few deep breaths to let this feeling subside, and then take time to read it through carefully.

Make absolutely sure you have read and understood each question. This is specially necessary for *either/or* questions, or those asking for a given number of examples, or those asking you to deal with a number of separated parts to a question.

(b) Try to keep to your allotted time for the questions you choose. You have a total of three hours for the whole paper. Allow half an hour for writing, in each case. Do not get carried away on one question where you know hundreds of relevant facts; you *may* get almost full marks for that question, but it is not worth running out of time for other questions.

(c) In your choice, go for safe (for you) topics which you feel confidently knowledgeable about. Students on unsafe ground too easily drift into 'waffle', repetition and even statements which do not make sense.

(d) Your plan should consist of a list of brief headings. Use these headings in the answer to make paragraphs on different points, and if a point needs illustrating, do so once, not several times. After you have completed the answer to your satisfaction, you can cross out this plan.

(e) Try not to re-phrase or repeat the question in full several times. For instance, do not keep writing 'Another reason why a child newly admitted to day nursery may feel strange and unhappy during his first few days could be that . . .' If you always relate your points directly to what you are asked you will not go off at a tangent.

(f) If you are asked to draw on your own experience, be concise. Use different children, or activities, or whatever you are writing about, to illustrate different points you are making. Do not be tempted to write in great detail about one particular child's behaviour only.

(g) Be precise and specific. Vague statements such as 'Construction play helps mental, physical and social development' won't do; make your meaning crystal clear. 'For instance', 'for example', and 'such as' ought to be the most used phrases in your writing. Every sentence you write should add something new and positive to the answer. You will not have time for elaborate introductory or concluding paragraphs, so don't waste time trying to write them.

(h) If the question asks you to 'list', do so. If it asks you to describe or relate 'briefly', then be brief. If you are running out of time, lists or headings and note-form writing may become unavoidable in other answers as well; this is quite acceptable if clearly written.

(i) Stay calm and muster all your thoughts just as if you were writing in essay form. If you have time left over at the end, you can always add to an answer you skimped on earlier, but be sure to make quite clear that it is, for instance, 'Question No. 7 continued'. Try to leave time to read through your whole paper; you may spot silly errors or vital omissions which could prevent you from gaining valuable marks.

6. After the examination

When you come out of the exam, do not enter into morbid 'post mortems' with your friends, as this could depress you.

GOOD LUCK!

EXAMPLE 1 OF A MULTIPLE CHOICE PAPER

1. What is the optimum age to test a baby's hearing by distraction methods?

   (a) five months
   (b) seven months
   (c) ten months
   (d) fifteen months

2. What is the earliest age a child can understand 'no'?

   (a) three months
   (b) nine months
   (c) fifteen months
   (d) twenty-four months

3. Is a ten-month old baby expected to be able to:

   (a) hold a conversation?
   (b) build two or three bricks into a tower?
   (c) sit alone and stand with support?
   (d) scribble with a pencil?

4. What is the best aid for a baby when he is learning to walk?

   (a) a baby-walker
   (b) a room containing stable furniture
   (c) well-fitting shoes
   (d) thick pile carpet on floor

5. Milk lacks one ingredient to make the perfect balanced food. Is it:

   (a) vitamin A?
   (b) carbohydrate?
   (c) iron?
   (d) vitamin D?

6. A baby is constipated:

   (a) if he fails to have his bowels open every day
   (b) if he strains and goes red when having his bowels open
   (c) if he passes hard, painful stools
   (d) if he passes large, bulky stools

7. What is the commonest form of malnutrition in Britain?

   (a) kwashiorkor
   (b) obesity
   (c) rickets
   (d) anaemia

8. A baby of three months is found to be very cold in his cot. Which is the best way to warm him?

   (a) Wrap him in blankets and surround him with hot water bottles.
   (b) Put him in a very warm bath.
   (c) Raise room temperature, remove blankets and cuddle him.
   (d) Give him a warm bottle of milk.

9. If a baby vomits curdled milk it indicates that:

   (a) the milk must have been in the stomach for a time
   (b) the milk must have been sour
   (c) the baby's stomach must be upset
   (d) the baby must be ill

10. Which of the following conditions can be detected in a baby before his birth?

   (a) spina bifida
   (b) dislocated hips
   (c) cystic fibrosis
   (d) phenylketonuria

11. Which of the following conditions is due to a genetic defect?

   (a) poliomyelitis
   (b) muscular dystrophy
   (c) dislocated hips
   (d) tonsillitis

12. The Guthrie test is used for detecting:

   (a) congenital dislocated hips
   (b) phenylketonuria
   (c) rubella
   (d) thyroid malfunction

13. What is the commonest cause of vomiting in a baby?

   (a) infection
   (b) genetic defect
   (c) allergy to milk
   (d) obstruction in the digestive tract

14. Head lice are more likely to be found in hair:

(a) which is rarely washed
(b) which is washed daily
(c) which is rarely combed
(d) which contains scurf

15. Natural fibres are best for baby's clothing because they:

(a) wash easily
(b) are absorbent
(c) are cheap
(d) are non-iron

16. Which baby is most likely to need an iron supplement during the first six months of life?

(a) light-for-dates baby
(b) pre-mature baby
(c) breast-fed baby
(d) bottle-fed baby

17. A child of three years is shivery and his temperature is 39°C. What treatment should be given whilst waiting for doctor?

(a) Wrap him in blankets.
(b) Cuddle him.
(c) Give him a hot drink.
(d) Put him in a cool bath.

18. A child is found to be suffering from rickets. This is caused by lack of:

(a) protein
(b) vitamin C
(c) vitamin D
(d) iron

19. Why does a baby of nine months put toys into his mouth?

(a) because he is teething
(b) because he thinks it is food
(c) because he wants to feel them
(d) because he likes the taste

20. Which of the following symptoms need urgent medical attention in a child of any age?

(a) earache
(b) sore throat
(c) vomiting
(d) crying

21. 'Cephalopod' is a word which can be applied to:

(a) a prehistoric monster in which infant-age children are usually interested
(b) a disease involving enlargement of the head
(c) the name given to the large human head drawn by young children
(d) the name of a character in a well-known children's book series

22. If a student were told that a toddler in her care was at the echolalia stage, she should conclude that this referred to:

(a) an aspect of behaviour
(b) an aspect of language development
(c) an aspect of hearing development
(d) an aspect of singing ability

23. Children should be involved in clearing up after play activities chiefly because:

(a) it is very tedious for the adults to do it all
(b) it trains children to take responsibility for their own actions
(c) it keeps children occupied for quite a long time
(d) Nursery nurses and teachers are not trained to be servants

24 Which of the following is NOT a natural play material?

(a) clay
(b) dough
(c) water
(d) sand

25. TACTILE means:

(a) something to do with the sense of touch
(b) something to do with all the senses
(c) something to do with being tactful
(d) something to do with textiles

26. Which of the following pieces of apparatus would be most likely to encourage co-operation in the under-threes?

(a) a rocker seesaw
(b) a baby walker
(c) a swing
(d) a large ball

27. Which of the following is essential if children are to be allowed to enjoy a paddling pool?

(a) constant supervision by an adult
(b) stimulating equipment
(c) enough space and time
(d) sunny weather

28. A four-year-old who has been painting a beautiful picture suddenly daubs the whole thing in black. The adult should:

(a) say 'What a shame, I was going to put that up on the wall.'
(b) suggest he begins again, and this time watch him closely to prevent repetition
(c) cross-question him about why he did it
(d) accept his action without comment

29. Cookery is a learning experience for the under-fives. Which one of the combinations (a) to (d) below gives the mathematical/ scientific concepts or skills that children are likely to meet most frequently in the process of cookery?

1. measurement of capacity
2. passing of time
3. effects of heat on raw substance
4. learning to read recipes
5. learning standard units of weight
6. measurement of length
7. recognition of familiar ingredients
8. need for accuracy

(a) 1, 2, 3 (b) 2, 4, 6 (c) 2, 3, 8 (d) 5, 7, 8

30. For which group of children might you appropriately make a demonstration clay 'coil' pot?

(a) three-to-four-year-olds who had run out of ideas
(b) three-to-five-year-olds who had never handled clay before
(c) any age children
(d) a group of top infants

31. Four-year-olds are enthusiastically playing doctors and hospitals in the converted Home Corner, examining each other's bodies. This probably denotes that:

(a) they have hang-ups about sex
(b) they can indulge in acceptable masturbation
(c) they are expressing normal curiosity about bodies
(d) they are trying to find out where they came from

32. Here is a list of equipment – bucket, ladle, colander, spade, rake. For which sort of play would these items be most suitable?

(a) clay
(b) gardening
(c) sand
(d) water

33. 'It encourages first-hand experience in three-dimensional shape, promotes resourcefulness, and often involves parents in supplying the basic necessities.' This description could best be applied to:

(a) junk modelling
(b) water play
(c) construction sets
(d) sand play

34. Which musical instrument would be the most appropriate for introducing ideas of rhythm to young children?

(a) shakers
(b) xylophone
(c) recorder
(d) piano

35. Which statement can be correctly applied to the introduction of music to young children?

(a) The adult should have a good singing voice.
(b) The adult should convey enthusiasm and confidence.
(c) The adult should be able to read music.
(d) The adult should have wide knowledge of music.

36. Three-year-old twins in nursery class communicate very seldom with other children or adults. The most likely reason is that:

(a) they were born prematurely and are behind in all the normal milestones of development
(b) they resent the presence of strangers
(c) insufficient approaches are being made to them by other people
(d) they have devised their own self-sufficient means of communication

37. Which of the following questions would be most likely to promote meaningful conversation with three to five year olds, based on a picture about a harvest scene?

(a) 'What can you see?'
(b) 'How many pieces of machinery can you see?'
(c) 'What is happening here?'
(d) 'How does a combine harvester work?'

38. The most appropriate way of celebrating Guy Fawkes night with five to seven year olds at infants school would be to:

(a) let them organise their own party
(b) tell them the full story of the Gunpowder Plot
(c) ask them to write a story about someone else being blown up
(d) initiate the making of a collage picture of bonfire and guy

39. Templates and tracing activities are often seen in pre-school establishments. They are most suitable for:

(a) two-year-olds
(b) three-year-olds
(c) four-year-olds
(d) all ages

40. The particular value of templates and tracing is that they:

(a) develop appreciation of artistic ideas
(b) encourage children to copy exactly
(c) help children develop concentration skills
(d) help children develop pencil control

41. A ten-month-old child wakes screaming an hour after being put to bed. Should she be:

(a) left to cry it out
(b) brought downstairs for a cuddle
(c) scolded and told to go to sleep
(d) comforted in her cot and accompanied until she falls asleep

42. What is the best way to deal with a three-month-old baby who is always crying, although the doctor can find nothing wrong?

(a) play with him all the time
(b) provide him with mobiles to look at
(c) let him cry in a room alone
(d) carry him around with you

43. What is the best answer to a four-year-old's question of 'Where do babies come from?'

(a) full description of sexual act and pregnancy
(b) 'You'll know when you are older'
(c) 'The stork brings them'
(d) 'They grow in mummies' tummies'

44. Acceptable discipline for young children involves:

(a) corporal punishment
(b) many reprimands and restraints
(c) more or less completely free expression
(d) a framework of what is and is not permissible

45. A three-year-old is most likely to learn the social graces if:

(a) they are the customary habits of his family
(b) he is constantly reminded of 'pleases' and 'thank you's'
(c) his minders try to compensate for lack of social graces at home
(d) all adults recognise that social graces will develop naturally later on

46. To which of the following situations does the term 'sibling rivalry' apply?

(a) two friends quarrelling over a toy
(b) mother and child competing for husband's/father's attention
(c) brother and sister co-operating over a household task
(d) brother and sister competing to please parent over a household task

47. Personality traits such as leadership and independence can usually be seen in a child by the time he is:

(a) one year
(b) two years
(c) three years
(d) four years

48. A four-year-old at infant school makes no effort to undress or dress himself for P.E. sessions. His mother has probably not fully met his need for:

(a) tender loving care
(b) growing independence
(c) manipulative skills
(d) asserting his own importance

49. A student is told that a four-year-old in her care is very gregarious. This means:

(a) he has a very large appetite
(b) he loves companionship
(c) he is a loner
(d) he is spiteful

50. 'Rough and tumble' play with father helps the toddler to:

(a) stick up for himself
(b) use more force than he likes to with his mother
(c) find out who is boss in his family
(d) express aggressive impulses legitimately

51. The mother of an eighteen-month-old child sits down near him at a quiet moment of the day, to continue reading an enthralling book of her own. The child is likely to:

(a) respect her need for quiet and privacy
(b) scream the place down
(c) remain unaware of her action
(d) recover her full attention by some means

52. The most appropriate way of celebrating Hallowe'en with nursery age children would be:

(a) for the adult to tell scary stories of witches and spells
(b) for the adult to draw witches, masks etc. and children cut them out and play with them
(c) adult and children transform the whole room into a witches' den
(d) for the adult to tell funny stories about witches

53. Most children discover the power of the negative between the ages of one and two. This is because:

(a) it's easier to say 'no' than 'yes'
(b) they enjoy upsetting people
(c) they are asserting their own independence
(d) it's a child's way of getting his own back on his mother

54. Two small children are sitting on the floor, playing haphazardly with bricks. There is little interaction, but after a few minutes one child shuffles on his bottom round the other, stares, touches him, and tries to snatch a brick. These children are likely to be aged:

(a) three to four months
(b) nine to ten months
(c) sixteen to eighteen months
(d) eighteen to twenty months

55. A mosque is:

(a) a Moslem place of worship
(b) a Jewish place of worship
(c) a Hindu shrine
(d) an Indian head-dress

56. Cases of anaemia may be seen among Rastafarian children because:

(a) their parents don't believe in breast-feeding
(b) their parents don't believe in iron tablets
(c) their parents follow a vegetarian diet
(d) their parents don't believe in vitamins

57. Some Asian children in 'your' nursery group are from a family who came to this country in the last decade. You hear staff refer sometimes to the long, nightmare journey experienced by this family. They are most likely to be:

(a) Ugandan Asians
(b) Iranians
(c) West Indians
(d) Vietnamese

58. What do you understand by Divali?

(a) The Hindu Festival of Light
(b) Jewish celebration of the Passover
(c) dress worn by Moslems
(d) a Sikh religious ritual

59. A baby's temperament is affected by:

(a) factors in his environment, and methods of handling
(b) genetic characteristics only
(c) genetic characteristics, factors in his environment, and methods of handling
(d) genetic characteristics, and social class of the family

60. A student sees a Pakistani mother reading a story to a group of children at nursery in her own language. It can be assumed that:

(a) the nursery staff are befriending her
(b) she doesn't know much English
(c) she is co-operating in mother-tongue work
(d) the children listening won't understand much

61. There appear to be several children with the same second name of Singh in a nursery class. It can be assumed that their families:

(a) are all related
(b) are Moslem
(c) are Hindu
(d) are Sikh

62. Which of the following traditional stories would you avoid in planning a theme for a group of nursery children including several Moslems?

(a) Goldilocks
(b) Cinderella
(c) Red Riding Hood
(d) The Three Little Pigs

63. Which book would you include in the book corner for a group of nursery children containing many from Caribbean families?

(a) *Cooking Caribbean Dishes*
(b) *The Backgrounds of our Ethnic Minority Groups*
(c) *Little Black Sambo*
(d) *Whistle for Willie*

64. Which of the following is responsible for registration of child minders?

(a) Social Services
(b) Health Authority
(c) Social Security
(d) Environmental Health Service

65. At what age is it legal for a person to be left in charge of a child under five years?

(a) twelve years
(b) fourteen years
(c) sixteen years
(d) eighteen years

66. Which condition must a pregnant woman fulfil in order to qualify for the right to return to her job after the baby is born?

(a) to work until she is six months pregnant
(b) to have worked for an employer for one year previous to pregnancy
(c) to return to work within a year of birth
(d) to have worked for her employer for two years

67. Which of the following people get automatic exemption from road tax on their car?

(a) a disabled person
(b) a person receiving Mobility Allowance
(c) a person using a car for his daily work in the Health Service
(d) a person receiving Family Income Supplement

68. The Invalid Care Allowance is given to someone who gives up work to care for a severely disabled person. Which of the following people can NOT claim?

(a) married women living with their husbands
(b) people who are already unemployed
(c) close relatives of the disabled
(d) people on Supplementary Benefit

69. Compassionate Friends are:

(a) a teenage equivalent of Alcoholics Anonymous
(b) a support group for teenage mothers
(c) a support group for separated and divorced adults
(d) a support group for bereaved parents

70. A father stays at home and looks after the couple's two young children while his wife works full-time. This is an example of:

(a) reversal of roles
(b) lack of motivation
(c) a tragic effect of unemployment
(d) trying to make ends meet

71. Which of the following attributes would you rate most highly for an intending registered child minder?

1. caring attitude
2. firmness
3. good business head
4. professional training
5. a large home
6. co-operation of her own family
7. awareness of domestic hazards
8. expensive play equipment

(a) 2, 3, 4 (b) 1, 6, 7 (c) 5, 7, 8 (d) 1, 3, 8

72. The welfare state became a reality in Great Britain during which period?

(a) 1860–1872
(b) 1900–1916
(c) 1939–1945
(d) 1944–1951

73. What do you understand by the term Home Visitors?

(a) an alternative name for Health Visitors
(b) an alternative name for Social Workers
(c) Nursery/School staff who liaise with children's families
(d) Children's officers from the NSPCC

74. The grandfather of a child to whom a qualified nursery nurse is a nanny begins giving her boxes of chocolates and expensive perfume. The nanny would be wise to:

(a) refuse firmly to accept anything
(b) accept them appreciatively
(c) explain that she is being paid for her job and cannot accept anything extra
(d) complain about his behaviour to the mother

75. Which attributes should be rated most highly by prospective employers of a nanny?

1. tact
2. outspokenness
3. assertiveness
4. adaptability
5. authoritativeness
6. stickability
7. meekness
8. intensity

(a) 2, 3, 4 (b) 1, 6, 8 (c) 4, 5, 7 (d) 1, 4, 6

76. A nanny is told by her employer, the child's mother, that she – the mother – must not do any household chores that might result in broken fingernails, as she is a photographer's model. The reaction of the nanny should be:

(a) to accept this as part of the reason she is there in the job
(b) to conclude that the employer is lazy and making excuses
(c) to insist that chores are fairly shared between them both
(d) to suggest that she wears false nails

77. Many 'first' nanny jobs do not last longer than a year. This is mainly because:

(a) the family grows up and its needs change
(b) the nanny was not confident enough
(c) inevitable personality clashes occur between employers and nanny
(d) expectations of nanny and employer are different

78. Evening social functions at nursery/infant school are valuable mainly because:

(a) they make welcome profits for the school fund
(b) it is easier to discuss children when they are not around
(c) parents can say how *they* want to see the school run
(d) staff and parents can meet socially at an informal level

79. Two students are going home on a bus from their day nursery placement and one begins talking to the other in a critical way about staff at nursery. Her friend would be advised to:

(a) say she does not agree with this point of view
(b) pointedly change the subject
(c) continue the conversation in low voices
(d) check that no-one from nursery is on the bus before continuing the conversation

80. A nursery nurse student is told that 'her' nursery class teacher is planning an outing with a group of three-to-four year olds to a nearby docks. Her first reaction should be to:

(a) try to persuade the teacher to choose somewhere which sounds safer
(b) start doing a project on docks and shipping
(c) ask the teacher how she can fit into this interest
(d) collect all the information she can on docks and shipping

EXAMPLE 1 OF AN ESSAY PAPER

You will have three hours for the whole paper, and must answer one question from each of Sections A, B, C and D. The maximum marks for these are shown in the right hand column.

SECTION A

		Marks
A1	Describe the appearance and behaviour of a four-year-old child who you have observed is tired.	8
	What reasons could there be for this condition?	6
	What steps could be taken to help him?	6
	or	
A2	Why is ante-natal care so important?	10
	State what statutory services are available to the pregnant woman.	10

SECTION B

B1	Select a book you consider suitable for children aged three to five.	4
	Describe how you would introduce it to a small group, linking it with their interests and experience.	16
	or	
B2	'Play is the business of childhood.'	
	Comment on this statement.	12
	Has urban living seriously encroached upon children's play possibilities?	8

SECTION C

C1	A child is finding difficulty in conforming to a standard of behaviour acceptable within his day nursery. What can the adults do to help?	20

or

C2 Describe some of the possible difficulties facing children of EITHER non-English speaking parents OR a minority group (of your choice). 10
Outline some of the practical ways in which the nursery nurse may help. 10

SECTION D

D1 Imagine that you are resident nanny in a private home where you are in charge of a child aged three years. The parents are working from 9.00 a.m. to 5.00 p.m.
In this situation describe how would you try to meet the needs of:
(a) the child 8
(b) the parents 6
(c) yourself 6

D2 A letter printed in a newspaper deplores the fact that a local authority proposes to spend more money on nursery education, in an area where there is already much play-group provision.
ANSWER this letter 20

Here is one way in which a good candidate might answer Sections A, B, C and D.

SECTION A

Reasons for choice

I would choose A1, the essay on the tired child, because I have had experience of this in one of my practical situations – a day nursery. Many children arrived at nursery tired and we often had discussions on the best way to help them. So I have theoretical knowledge from my health lectures, together with practical experience.

Looking at A2, I notice that half the marks are for statutory services available. I am rather doubtful about my accuracy on this subject. I could probably write a lot about why ante-natal care is important, but would only get five marks at the most, so it is not worth wasting the time and effort on it.

A1: Plan of my answer

APPEARANCE:	Heavy dull eyes, dark rings pale inactive dull uninterested slow miserable		
REASONS:	*Lack of sleep* hate bedtime too much TV not enough room	*Fears* dark bed-wetting marital quarrels insecurity	*Illness*
HELP:	Talk to parents Find reasons Give nap in day		

Essay

A healthy four-year-old is a lively, active child and life for him is a constant adventure. He is alert and receptive and full of curiosity, asking questions and absorbing information.

In a group of such children the tired child will stand out, both in appearance and activity. He is usually pale and heavy-eyed, his eyes appearing dull and expressionless, with dark rings under them. He moves slowly and is reluctant to do extra activity.

A tired child tends to regress in behaviour and to act like a much younger child. He may become withdrawn and solitary or may cling to the nearest adult, whining and sucking his thumb. His reactions will be slow and clumsy because tiredness affects co-ordination.

Most tired children are easily upset by any minor setback, and cannot tolerate frustration. Instead of waking naturally in the morning, full of enthusiasm for the new day, this child will need to be roused and may be reluctant to get up at all.

The most obvious cause of tiredness is a lack of sleep, but there are many reasons why a child may not be getting enough sleep. In some cases it is simply because the child is allowed to stay up too late. Many children look upon bedtime as a time of banishment from all the 'fun' of adult life downstairs, and will take advantage of any hesitation or uncertainty on the part of the parents to postpone bedtime. The constant request for drinks of water is a very familiar ploy.

Some parents give up the struggle and allow the children to stay up to watch television. Consequently, most teachers and nursery nurses are familiar with the Monday morning syndrome, i.e., extreme tiredness in young children every Monday morning because of late nights at the weekend.

Some children have late nights throughout the week as well, so that they are constantly tired. These children are often over-stimulated by unsuitable television programmes so that when they do eventually go to bed it takes a long time for sleep to come, thus aggravating the problem. Other reasons for a late bedtime include the child being kept up late as company for a parent, either in a one-parent family or where the father works late and the child stays up to see his dad.

Families who live in limited accommodation often have bedtime problems. If the family lives in just one room then it is difficult for the child to fall asleep in the evening when the parents want to talk or watch television. Some children have to share a bedroom with their parents and/or brothers and sisters, and this can be very disturbing.

Even children who are put to bed at a reasonable time may have difficulty in sleeping. There are many possible reasons for this, ranging from fear of the dark to emotional insecurity. At four years a child has a rapidly developing imagination which may lead to sleeplessness or nightmares.

If there are marital problems or family rows the child may react by being wakeful at night, especially if he is afraid his mother will leave him. Another reason for wakefulness at this age could be a fear of wetting the bed. Some four-year-olds will not have attained night bladder control, and even if they have control, accidents can still occur. If he is treated with punishment or scorn the child may try to stay awake in case he needs to go to the lavatory.

Wakefulness also occurs in children who have an erratic daily routine. They may lack exercise and fresh air, or may be bored and unstimulated, and consequently not ready for sleep at bedtime. A child who is physically under par, or who is developing an infection, can be a poor sleeper too.

The most obvious step to take to help a tired four-year-old would be to try to discover the reason and to put it right. First, observation of the child may reveal that he is ill. If he has other signs and symptoms, such as a raised temperature or a rash, then medical aid should be sought as soon as possible.

In any case, the child should be examined by a doctor to check whether there is physical reason for the tiredness which can be corrected. For example, if he is undernourished then ensuring he has good balanced meals during the day may be sufficient to aid sleep and prevent tiredness.

In the nursery or nursery school the tired child can be given the opportunity to sleep during the day, and observation of the child and a discussion with the parents may elicit the reason for his tiredness. If it is due to a housing problem or to a one-parent situation, then there is no reason why the child should not be given a sleep-period each day to enable him to cope with late bedtimes.

But if the cause is too much television then the nursery nurse should tactfully explain to the parents the need for early bedtimes. If the nursery nurse points out how tired the child is, and how much of the school activities he misses because of this, it may help to persuade the mother of the need for the child to sleep longer. Sometimes explaining to the parents that some four-year-old 'bad' behaviour, such as wetting the bed, is normal can be sufficient to relieve the pressure on the child and prevent false expectations from the parents.

A basic routine at home helps to give a four-year-old child a feeling of security. He needs regular periods of activity and rest, punctuated by mealtimes. An unhurried bedtime routine is soothing and induces sleep; therefore his day should be organised so that the approach to bedtime is a 'winding down' period.

If the nursery nurse should discover that a particular home problem, such as a new baby, is worrying him then she may be able to relieve his anxiety by reading him stories about similar situations and by giving him extra attention.

This specimen answer first appeared in *Nursery World*, the baby and child care magazine.

SECTION B

Reasons for choice

I would avoid question B2. As it is such a big subject, I might easily ramble, or go over time. I am not sure I altogether understand what is wanted in the second part. My choice will therefore be B1.

B1: Plan of my answer

1. Description of chosen book. Reasons for suitability. Preparation.
2. Create receptive atmosphere
3. Manner of telling – voices, varying speed, tone, etc.; humour, suspense, relief, chance to identify with, handling of interruptions. Gentle end.
4. 'Rounding off' time.

Essay

At my last nursery school placement, I really enjoyed my regular story sessions with the children and got to know their tastes well.

The Tiger who came to Tea, written and illustrated by Judith Kerr (Collins), would offer this age group a chance to step in and out of the worlds of reality and fantasy; they can do this with complete ease and acceptance.

The book tells the tale of a benevolent but greedy tiger's visit to an ordinary household. The happenings are quite impossible, but are nonetheless rooted in reality, in the sense that the tiger acts in an exaggerated, yet recognisably human way. No supernatural beings or magic are involved. Three to five-year-olds would identify with Sophie, the little girl of the household, and would recognise the other figures – such as parents and trades people. There is no strong characterisation, but at this stage children do not require this. The action moves swiftly, and the few lines of text on each page relate directly to the illustrations.

There is a slight element of fear and suspense – the tiger *does* look large! But there is plenty of humour in his antics. The domestic setting would be recognisable to children, and this would counteract any fear experienced.

The story would probably generate satisfying feelings of condemnation and self-righteousness at the tiger's monumental appetite, and the resulting devastation. There is a satisfactorily happy ending when Father suggests that the family go to a café for tea; a final, reassuring note, tells the reader that the tiger never returns.

Having read the story silently a couple of times, I would gather my group in a comfortable and contained setting, probably the Book Corner, and I would seat myself on a child's low chair so that all the children could see and hear me clearly. To help settle them into a receptive mood, I would suggest we played a short game of 'sleeping lions'. While they were still 'sleeping', I would link the idea of lions and tigers, and announce that today, I had for them a story about a tiger who did something 'very strange'.

Having captured the interest and curiosity of my audience, I would begin the story, making sure that I held the book open in front of the children so that all could see and enjoy the colourful and entertaining pictures. I would be so familiar with the text that a sideways view of each page would allow me to follow it. Giving the children enough time to take in each new character and development, I would make the most of pauses, and drop my voice to a whisper at moments of suspense.

I would try to 'weave' in the children's interjections such as 'I know what milkmen . . .', 'My Dad has some keys like that . . .' But each time, I would firmly bring them back to the next step in the story so that interjectors did not have the chance to vie with each other. I would adopt a funny, deep voice for the tiger, and leave enough time for the 'ooh's' and 'aah's' and giggles at his size and antics. In the middle of the story, where the author has pictured the tiger cuddled up to Sophie, wondering what else he can find to eat, I would pause slightly longer, to allow the irony and possibilities of the situation to be assimilated by the older children.

In the unlikely event of the children's interest waning at the list of food and drink consumed, I would quicken my pace and emphasise particular words to give an impression of a series of mini-climaxes. Throughout the story I would try to maintain eye contact with the children. At the point of the tiger's departure, I would pause and allow my tone of voice to become more matter-of-fact; this would probably accord with the relief felt by my audience.

The better to enable my audience to appreciate Daddy's bright idea, I would register concern in my voice and in my face at Mummy's dilemma over the empty pantry.

I would help the children savour the unfamiliar thrill of going out at night and seeing street lights shining, as this is especially well illustrated. I hope they would enjoy imagining the taste of Sophie's favourite foodstuffs – 'sausage and chips and ice-cream'. At this point there would probably be more interruptions about the favourite foods of my audience, but I would try to hold their attention until the end of the story. I would offer the last sentences slowly and in a manner of finality. I would then pause to allow the spell to fade gently. Requests such as 'read it again', or 'read us another one', I would interpret as compliments, but would resist.

On how much to talk about the story afterwards, I would take my cue from the children. I would certainly not cross-question them to test their comprehension, but if they seemed eager to stay with the subject, I would ask some open-ended questions about their visits to zoos or cafés, or even 'What do you think you would do if a tiger came to tea with you?' When this discussion came to a natural end, I would round off the session with a song such as, 'I went to the animal fair.'

This specimen answer first appeared in *Nursery World*, the baby and child care magazine.

SECTION C

Reasons for choice

I would avoid question C2, as I have had very little practical experience of working with non-English speaking families, or minority groups. This means that I shall choose C1.

C1: Plan of my answer

- Reasons for behaviour
- Start where he's at
- 1:1 relationship and affection and approval
- Positive self-image
- Suitable play
- Handling tantrums
- Avoiding all negatives
- Preventive measures
- Framework of security

Essay

Knowing the nature of a child's troubled background is the first step in understanding him and treating him with insight and sensitive care. If, for instance, he has grown up with parental models of violence and physical and verbal abuse, it is small wonder that this becomes his natural means of interaction and self-assertion.

Nursery nurses must accept a child as he is and aim to build slowly from that point. They should retain realistic expectations of his conduct, make their demands on him simple and clear, and also practise consistency themselves and as a staff. Inconsistency will open the way for confusion and anti-social behaviour on the child's part.

A one-to-one relationship with one nursery nurse is essential for a disturbed child's settling process. He must discover that he can trust and depend upon that person's kind but firm manner; he may then gradually reveal to her both the vulnerable and the likeable sides of his character. As the nursery nurse learns his foibles and interests, and works in harmony with these, understanding and affection between child and nursery nurse grow steadily. From this one secure relationship, the child will gradually work outwards to include other adults and children.

Much can be done to build up a child's positive self-image. Frequent use of his name is a starting point. Use of first and surname, spoken in firm tones, can also be effective; it clearly pinpoints to whom the remark is being addressed, yet reinforces the child's identity.

Tasks, play activities and social situations in which the child can succeed and be accepted must be stage managed. Helping the adult in many different kinds of chores, such as wiping down tables, giving out 'snacks', may make the child feel important and grown-up.

Praise should be whole-hearted. Warm and meaningful comment should be made when, for instance, he spends a longer than usual time tackling a puzzle, or makes a small sharing gesture.

A folder or scrap album can be kept, especially for the child's pictures and art work. This, again, underlines the child's worth as an individual and also gives rise to more useful one to one times with 'his' nursery nurse. Themes on 'faces', 'ourselves when babies', 'photographs' will all help this child see himself clearly, in a positive light.

As a relaxed trust develops, the child will probably respond to shows of affection, and physical contact. A lap cuddle or game, an arm round as the nursery nurse shares a book with him, are calming and reassuring. Holding hands, and eye contact are useful restraining tactics in fraught moments. Because he may lack tender physical contact at home, hairdressing play can be a substitute for this.

Other beneficial forms of play will include: vigorous outdoor activity on apparatus, wheeled vehicles, using large spaces; woodwork for channelling aggression; clay for mess, thumping and banging; dough (pink dough resembling flesh is particularly good for 'pinchers' and 'biters'); Blocks for crashing down; sand for vigorous digging and legitimate destruction; paper tearing and cutting. Water play can be soothing.

In the Home Corner, the child can re-enact domestic scenes, thus externalising and coming to terms with the puzzling world of adults.

He can treat dolls either harshly, or lovingly, as his mood dictates. There should be sufficient exciting items, such as dressing-up hats, to avoid much quarrelling over these.

Despite all these measures, there are bound to be lapses. It is up to the nursery nurse to try and structure the day so that situations likely to precipitate trouble are avoided, or minimised. For instance, boredom caused by keeping children waiting too long at an empty table for their dinner, or crammed in a story setting, incites anti-social behaviour.

Other things to avoid are confrontations with the child, of the 'I'm waiting here until you say you are sorry' variety. Someone has to back down in that situation; if it is the child (unlikely) it does nothing for his self-image; if it is the nursery nurse, her authority with the group is diminished.

Staff should also avoid labelling a child out loud, to each other, or even mentally as, for instance, 'The holy terror of Green Room'. Children quickly sense a reputation like this and usually enjoy living up to it.

To keep using the word 'naughty' and saying 'no' and 'stop it' is negative and unconstructive. Distraction and diversionary tactics at an early stage of potential trouble is much more appropriate. Under-threes are quite easily distracted. Over-threes can often be flattered into accepting an invitation to help a nursery nurse perform a job.

Disapproval, and refusal to tolerate certain sorts of behaviour must, of course, be expressed at times. Often a 'more in sorrow than in anger' approach is best. The child will want to retain the regard and affection of the nursery nurse. Reprimands should not be carried out in front of a group of children; a leading figure is tempted to play up to an audience.

There will be occasions when, for his own or other children's good, a child may need to be removed from a group. He should be kept within supervisory distance, and not be placed in a room on his own where he may totally lose control; nor should he be taken to the Officer-in-Charge's room, lest he comes to associate this with punishment.

At mealtimes, group times, story times, strategic placing of a disruptive child, so that the adult can extend a restraining hand when needed, has a helpful effect. Separation of pairs of disruptive children is advisable.

Swearing can be a problem. As far as possible it should be ignored; it may be the everyday language the child hears at home. However, if it is used deliberately to upset or startle, and if it is having a harmful effect on other children, or worrying parents, the child must be told firmly but unemotionally that he must not say those words.

Where practicable, acts of deliberate destruction should be rectified by the child, with the adult calmly and firmly supervising. This is a good lesson in experiencing the consequences of one's actions – as a mere matter of fact, not as punishment – and it plays a valuable part in the behaviour modification process.

However trying and exasperating he may be at times, staff dealing with a disturbed child should remain outwardly calm and in control, patient, tolerant and unshockable. Although he may constantly kick against it and see 'how far he can go', set boundaries of behaviour are required for his inner security, with the adult clearly seen as being in command of the situation.

This specimen answer first appeared in *Nursery World*, the baby and child care magazine.

SECTION D

Reasons for choice

I am hoping to become a nanny myself within a few weeks, so I have chosen D1, as this question is very relevant to my present thoughts.

I would avoid D2, as I am not in the habit of writing to newspapers.

D1: Plan of my answer

1. All-round needs of *child*
   Creating happy atmosphere and good relationship
   Typical daytime routines and activities
   Widening his social contacts
   Mental stimulation and language
   Domestic chores as starting points for stimulation
2. Keeping uppermost relationship between *parents* and child
   Tact and sensitivity in dealings with parents
   Confidentiality
3. Sensible régime for health, for *myself*
   Need for hobbies and friends, holidays
   Keeping up with world of child care
   Approach to job, interview, contract, etc. Minimum commitment.

Essay

As my charge would be 'mine' for the greater part of his waking day, and for at least part of the weekends, it would be up to me to try to fulfil his physical, social, emotional and intellectual needs in the way that good parents would do this. Within a framework of a regular, but flexible, routine, I would provide a balance of rest and exercise, vigorous play and quiet times, outdoors and indoors. I would give him well-balanced, attractively presented meals which we would enjoy together.

He would need a regular bath time, which should be an unhurried and pleasurable affair, and also washes at the beginning or end of the day, before meals, and after messy play. The child would be dependent on my maintaining a clean, healthy and *safe* environment in which he could feel free. Probably I would also attend to his clothing, keeping that in a good state of cleanliness and repair.

I would try to create a happy, stable atmosphere in which he could feel secure and not miss his parents' companionship and love too much. There would be many opportunities for fun, laughter and spontaneity. I would comfort him when he had a mishap or a disappointment. I would help him to come to terms with any fears or anxieties. Understanding the stage of development he has reached, I would avoid presenting him with tasks that were either too difficult or irksome, thus setting up frustration or resentment, or too easy, so that he became bored.

I would make the few 'rules of the house' – such as not going out of the garden gate – very clear, and explain the reasons for them simply, emphasising the love and care all adults feel for the child. In matters of discipline for misdemeanours, I would be guided by the parents' view, but in any case I would always make it plain that it was the deed of which I disapproved – not the child.

Through my being in the post, the child would already be extending his social contacts by making a relationship with an adult outside his family. I would build on this, with the parents' permission, by taking him to a local playgroup, and/or entertaining and being entertained by other nannies in the neighbourhood, caring for children of similar ages.

These measures would give the child his first taste of sharing toys, being polite to guests, and so on. True co-operative play will take time to evolve, but familiarisation with a group setting is a beginning.

I would enjoy meeting 'my' child's intellectual needs, especially furthering his fast-developing language skills. There would be many questions to answer in the course of the day. The interesting places to which I would take him – the local park, the zoo, the shops – would be particularly rich in talking points. All would stimulate his curiosity, and add to his knowledge of the world.

I would also enjoy introducing new books, songs, poems, action rhymes and games to him. I would watch selected children's television programmes with him, so helping him to become an active viewer by joining in responses, answering questions, or following up ideas offered.

Patiently, I hope, I should let him 'help' me about the house with the washing up, for instance, or dusting, gardening or making pastry. As there would probably be other domestic help employed, it would not matter if his 'help' and chatter delayed my completion of jobs. Frequently, I would join in his play, or be on hand to supply help, encouragement, and suggest further ideas. I would also provide him with improvised play materials, such as dressing-up clothes, squeezy bottle 'shakers' or paint pots. I would help him investigate further nature specimens found on our walks, or use them in art work, or collections.

I owe it to the parents not to supplant them in their child's eyes. In my conversation with the child I would frequently refer to them so as to keep them uppermost in his mind. I would be guided by them in all important matters of child-rearing, and I would hope that there would be such trust and mutual respect in our relationship that they could feel happy and confident at leaving the child in my sole charge.

I would keep the parents informed about the child's doings, progress and developments, funny sayings, etc. so that they could still feel in close touch with him. I would remember, however, that when they first come in tired from work, that may not be the best time to regale them with all the details.

I would ensure that the living rooms and kitchen were reasonably tidy and organised for their homecoming, so that they would not arrive home to a depressing shambles and an impression of incompetence. I might even cook some meals for them, or offer to babysit sometimes, and I would be adaptable about how I was recompensed for these extra tasks.

I would realise that having another person living under one's roof can bring problems of insufficient privacy, and I would be discreet about leaving them enough time alone with the child, or just alone together. Whatever private matters I learned about them or their lifestyle, I would treat with the utmost confidentiality.

Mine would be a demanding job, so I would ensure that I kept to a healthy régime, with sufficient exercise and sleep. I would need a fair amount of time off, and I would try to get right away from the work setting – my driving would be a help here. I would be greatly refreshed by contact with relatives and friends, keeping up my hobbies and interests, planning my next holiday.

I would try to avoid stagnating mentally – which can happen easily when one spends long hours solely in the company of a small child. I would read widely and keep up to date with new thinking on child-rearing or children's welfare. I would also try to stay well aware of the world outside and current affairs. I might go to evening classes, and perhaps study a foreign language, with an eye to future posts.

It is important that I should be happy in this post and derive job satisfaction from it. To increase the likelihood of this, I would visit the family initially, best of all for a residential weekend, so that we could really get to know one another and also clearly define my role. I would ask for a contract of employment to be drawn up, so that there was a formal agreement to uphold the boundaries of my responsibilities and conditions of service.

If all went according to plan, I would hope to stay in this job for at least a year, probably longer. This would ensure continuity of care for the child at a formative age. After all, his wellbeing is the whole purpose of my being employed by the family.

This specimen answer first appeared in *Nursery World*, the baby and child care magazine.

EXAMPLE 2 OF A MULTIPLE CHOICE PAPER

1. At what age should a child be trusted to cross the road alone?

   (a) three years
   (b) five years
   (c) six years
   ✓ (d) seven years

2. By the age of one year a baby should weigh:

   (a) 2 × birthweight
   ✓ (b) 3 × birthweight
   (c) 4 × birthweight
   (d) 5 × birthweight

3. What is the optimum age for a young child to be admitted to hospital for non-urgent surgery?

   (a) one year
   (b) one and a half years
   ✓ (c) three years
   (d) five years

4. What is the main reason for preventing decay in a child's first teeth?

   (a) It improves the child's appearance.
   (b) Any decay will spread to the permanent teeth.
   (c) It helps the child's facial development.
   ✓ (d) It prevents the permanent teeth being crowded.

5. Why is jaundice dangerous to a newborn baby?

   (a) It can cause liver damage.
   (b) It can cause the child to vomit all feeds.
   ✓ (c) It can cause brain damage.
   (d) It can cause a serious loss of fluid.

6. At what age do children play together?

   (a) one and a half years
   (b) two years
   (c) two and a half years
   ✓ (d) three years

7. A baby is able to chew lumpy food:

   (a) when he has teeth
   (b) when he is teething
   (c) from five months of age
   (d) from ten months of age

8. Children under two years of age should not be given skimmed milk because:

   (a) it is too thin
   (b) it is unsterile
   (c) it lacks protein
   (d) it lacks vitamins

9. What is the first symptom of scarlet fever?

   (a) sore throat
   (b) rash with raised spots
   (c) severe cough
   (d) diarrhoea

10. To calculate the amount of milk a baby under six months requires, which factor do you need to know?

    (a) the age of the baby
    (b) the condition of baby
    (c) the baby's appetite
    (d) the baby's weight

11. At what age should a child learn to swim?

    (a) as early as possible
    (b) when he wants to
    (c) after he starts school
    (d) when he understands the need

12. A premature baby is:

    (a) a baby weighing less than 2.500 kg
    (b) a baby born before thirty-eight weeks pregnancy
    (c) a baby born before thirty-two weeks pregnancy
    (d) a baby weighing less than 2.000 kg

13. Why is cow's milk NOT recommended for a baby under six months?

    (a) it contains too much fat
    (b) it contains too much salt
    (c) there is not enough protein
    (d) there is not enough carbohydrate

14. The APGAR score is a means of measuring:

(a) a child's condition at birth
(b) a child's developmental progress
(c) a child's rate of growth
(d) a child's general condition

15. A child with coeliac disease cannot eat food containing:

(a) gluten
(b) lactose
(c) fat
(d) vitamin D

16. The incubation period in an infectious disease is the length of time:

(a) a child should be isolated
(b) between the infection caught and symptoms developing
(c) a child is infectious
(d) between symptoms appearing and disease ending

17. If a fire breaks out in a day nursery, what is the first thing the staff should do?

(a) call the fire brigade
(b) close all the windows
(c) get the children out of the nursery
(d) try to put out the fire

18. Parents must register their baby within:

(a) two weeks
(b) four weeks
(c) six weeks
(d) twelve weeks

19. Which is the best way to prevent a child of one year falling down the stairs?

(a) do not allow him near the stairs
(b) put a gate at the bottom of the stairs
(c) teach him how to come down safely
(d) put a gate at the top and the bottom of the stairs

20. What is a Mongolian spot?

(a) a spot at the base of the spine in children of African blood
(b) a birthmark at the back of the neck
(c) a spot on the back of a Down's Syndrome child
(d) a birthmark on a child from Mongolia

21. Which of the following children's sentences is an example of telegraphese?

(a) Mum, mum, mum.
(b) I can see a car.
(c) Come quickly! I've found a spider!
(d) Daddy gone work.

22. Which of the following approaches would be the most appropriate for taking a music session with the under 5s?

(a) share selected instruments between different children to accompany each adult's song
(b) give each child an instrument and encourage all simultaneously to accompany a song
(c) demonstrate to the children a good example of skilled instrumental playing
(d) choose a few children with musical talent to play selected instruments

23. Which of the following musical instruments is most appropriate for introducing young children to melody?

(a) drum
(b) chime bars
(c) cymbals
(d) shakers

24. Music for the under-fives should be mainly:

(a) a participative experience
(b) a spectating and listening experience
(c) an aesthetic experience
(d) an auditory discrimination experience

25. Between six and nine months approximately, a baby makes determined efforts to communicate by:

(a) smiles, babbling and gestures
(b) words, smiles and gestures
(c) short sentences, smiles and gestures
(d) smiles and gestures only

26. Which one of the following substances is NOT a malleable play material?

(a) salt
(b) soil
(c) clay
(d) dough

27. A child, after making a recognisable clay model, asks about it the next day, and follows through the process of colouring it, glazing it, taking it home. The child is most likely to be:

(a) two to three years
(b) three to four years
(c) four to five years
✓(d) over five years

28. Dressing up hats are often worn by under-fives long after the imaginative game has finished. This is most probably because:

✓(a) a hat appears to be the most significant item in role change
(b) the child has forgotten to take it off
(c) the child is preventing another child from taking it
(d) hats are easier to manage than garments with fastenings

29. The particular value of involving small children in displays and activities on a 'springtime' theme is that:

(a) it offers stimulation of all the senses
(b) it can introduce ideas of Easter eggs, Easter bunnies
(c) it teaches them about the yearly cycle of nature
✓(d) it teaches them about the annual rebirth of natural life

30. Legs are often the next feature to appear after the 'big head' stage of drawing and painting in children of approximately two to four years. This is probably because:

(a) they are more important in life than arms
✓(b) small children are at 'leg level' in an adult world
(c) small children do not notice bodies or arms
(d) small children realise that arms and fingers are too difficult to attempt at this age

31. Colour recognition for the under-fives is best encouraged by:

(a) jigsaw puzzles
(b) nursery rhymes
(c) picture books
✓(d) bead threading

32. The moment of crash when children are building towers of blocks should be regarded as:

(a) trying to adults' nerves, but unavoidable
✓(b) a satisfying climax which encourages further building
(c) to be encouraged as it excites the children
(d) to be discouraged as it is a destructive act

33. Awareness of spatial relationships is best promoted by:

    (a) painting
    (b) clay and dough
    (c) block play
    (d) collage

34. 'Butterfly' painting offers a unique example of:

    (a) merging of attractive colours
    (b) colour recognition
    (c) pictorial composition
    (d) symmetry

35. 'Shop' play for all ages is likely to promote:

    (a) understanding of the money/goods transaction
    (b) familiarity with and recognition of coins
    (c) practice in adding up
    (d) practice in giving change

36. Play with toy farm animals for the under-fives will probably involve:

    (a) knowledge of food sources
    (b) knowledge of modern farming methods
    (c) the idea of sets
    (d) fantasy play

37. Which of the following 'props' would you NOT include in a hospital play kit for under-fives?

    (a) bandages
    (b) x-ray pictures
    (c) 'pretend' pills
    (d) scissors

38. Printing with a variety of fruit and vegetables is likely to encourage:

    (a) a good sense of humour
    (b) co-operative play
    (c) ideas of symmetry
    (d) awareness of pattern in nature

39. Water painting out of doors, with bucket and wide brush, might demonstrate to children:

    (a) condensation
    (b) water finding its own level
    (c) evaporation
    (d) displacement of water

40. A three-year-old brings to nursery a model letter box which can be used as a money box. This could offer a unique starting point for an educational project or theme on:

(a) the need to save for the future
✓(b) the role of the Post Office in communications
(c) the colour red
(d) writing letters

41. A student is told that a child has been in and out of 'care' most of his life, and has problems making relationships with other children and adults. The most likely reason is that:

(a) he has been on the receiving end of a non-accidental injury
(b) he did not have the chance as a baby to bond with his mother
(c) he has been neglected by foster parents
✓(d) he has been looked after by too many different people

42. A four-year-old could be said to be at an acceptable stage of social development if:

✓(a) he interacts satisfactorily with children and adults
(b) he practises good manners in all situations
(c) he is always one of a crowd of children
(d) he is always trying to make friends

43. Distraction is a useful method of dealing with which of the following situations?

(a) a two-year-old child in the throes of a temper tantrum
(b) a four-year-old child who is crying with earache
✓(c) a two-and-a-half-year-old child who is about to unravel knitting
(d) a three-year-old child who refuses to eat his dinner

44. A four-year-old at nursery seems frequently drawn towards clay, dough, woodwork, sand and other materials where he can cut, bang, pummel and destroy. You could safely assume that:

(a) he is a child given to moods
(b) there must be a problem at home
(c) he is naturally aggressive
✓(d) he needs to work out negative feelings

45. A four-year-old is starting infant school. The mother is making arrangements to meet him at the end of the day. She would be wise in the first instance to:

(a) join a rota of mothers who take it in turns to meet their children
(b) explain that his elder brother will be there as soon as he can after junior school
(c) ask the child what arrangements he would like
(d) be there promptly to meet him herself.

46. A child is upset at the idea of parting from his mother on his first day at nursery school. The staff should:

(a) urge the mother to say goodbye firmly and leave soon with minimal fuss
(b) invite the mother to stay as long as she likes, all day if she chooses
(c) involve both in an activity, then suggest mother says goodbye, promises to return, and leaves
(d) involve the child in an activity, then signal to the mother to slip away while the child is preoccupied

47. A nursery nurse is visiting friends. She observes an incident where a three-year-old has alternately rocked, kissed, and slyly pinched his ten-day-old sister. Which statement would make the best interpretation, if she were recording this incident?

(a) all small children display jealousy of new siblings
(b) given a few more months, he will probably grow out of this behaviour
(c) his parents cannot have sufficiently prepared him for baby's arrival
(d) he is experiencing the normal mixed and powerful emotions towards a baby sibling

48. When visiting the above family for the first time since the baby's birth, the student would be wise to:

(a) take neither child a present so as not to attach too much importance to the event
(b) take both children a present but let the child unwrap the baby's as well
(c) take only the older child a present to compensate for feelings of jealousy
(d) take the baby a present but give it privately to the mother

49. Which of the following would be a suitable birthday gift for a one-year-old boy?

(a) a baby walker
(b) Lego bricks
(c) a rattle and teething ring
(d) a 'push along' toy on wheels

50. A family of three boys, four years, five years and seven years, often fight one another for a toy. Would this be:

(a) normal sibling rivalry
(b) a sign of insecurity
(c) because the parents fight
(d) a sign of deprivation

51. A six-weeks-old baby is always crying, although the doctor can find nothing physically wrong. Which of the following would best help him:

(a) leave him to cry in a room with the door shut
(b) start him on cereals to fill him up
(c) carry him around with you in a baby sling
(d) give him mobiles to watch

52. A three-year-old rolls some pieces of red clay and, giggling self-consciously, calls to you to look at her 'pooh poohs'. Your best course of action would be to:

(a) pretend you have not heard her
(b) say 'No, they're sausages,' firmly
(c) distract her attention
(d) smile and watch

53. A child of three years is masturbating. Which is the best way to deal with it?

(a) ignore it and give him something else to do
(b) warn him that he will injure himself
(c) tell him to stop it at once
(d) tell him he is not allowed to do it

54. The best way to develop a child's self control and discipline is to:

(a) insist that he obeys at all times
(b) praise him for 'good' behaviour
(c) punish him for 'bad' behaviour
(d) make him say 'please' if he wants anything

55. A two-year-old girl has become very aggressive. Which sort of play would be helpful to her?

(a) Lego blocks
(b) small cars and a garage
✓(c) water play
(d) a tray jigsaw

56. A student nursery nurse is told that a number of children from Plymouth Brethren families attend her (placement) infant school. She can reasonably expect these children to:

(a) make frequent reference to their relatives in the West country
(b) be inter-related, one with another
✓ (c) be barred by their parents from taking part in assembly and religious festivals
(d) be influenced by their non-Christian parents in many subtle ways

57. The term 'common law' wife means:

(a) a divorcée living alone
(b) a woman who is engaged
(c) another man's wife
✓ (d) a woman living with a man as his wife

58. A qualified nursery nurse has been taken on by an Iranian family living in England. Which statement about her future life is most likely to be true?

(a) there will be language difficulties
(b) the children will resent her as an outsider
(c) they will be travelling abroad a good deal
✓ (d) there will be cultural differences for her to adjust to

59. Urdu and Hindi are:

(a) different types of garment
✓(b) languages spoken in the Indian sub-continent
(c) sacred places of pilgrimage for Hindus
(d) names of two Hindu gods

60. Ugandan Asians came to Britain in the 1970s in large numbers because:

✓ (a) they were made political refugees
(b) they thought their children would get a better education
(c) they had heard that British employment prospects were good
(d) they thought British people would be friendly

61. Ramadan means:

- (a) a period of fasting for Moslems
- (b) a temple of worship for Moslems
- (c) an Indian language
- (d) the Holy Book of Moslems

62. The term 'maternal grandmother' means:

- (a) a child's mother's mother
- (b) a motherly grandmother
- (c) a pregnant grandmother
- (d) a child's father's mother

63. If you were told that there were several travellers' families children in 'your' infant class, you could reasonably expect that:

- (a) their fathers are sales representatives
- (b) their fathers are in the Services
- (c) the families have lived abroad
- (d) the families live in mobile homes

64. P.A.N.N. stands for:

- (a) Prevention of Accidents to Nursery Nurses
- (b) Professionally Amalgamated Nursery Nurses
- (c) Professional Association of Nursery Nurses
- (d) Professional Association of Night Nurses

65. Registered child-minding is a valuable form of caring provision for the under-fives because:

- (a) it is cheaper for parents than employing a nanny
- (b) the child-minder can act as mother to a large group
- (c) it most resembles a good home setting
- (d) child-minders work longer hours than playgroups

66. A paediatrician is:

- (a) a medical officer
- (b) a doctor who specialises in children's diseases
- (c) a doctor who specialises in pregnancy
- (d) a doctor who specialises in feet

67. S.E.N. stands for:

- (a) Statistically Educationally Normal
- (b) Society of Enrolled Nurses
- (c) State Enrolled Nurse
- (d) Social and Environmental Nurse

68. Which child is *most* at risk from child abuse?

(a) the only child
(b) the first-born child
(c) the prematurely-born child
(d) the last-born child

69. Which of the following injuries in an eighteen-month-old boy would be indicative of non-accidental injury?

(a) scald on arm
(b) cigarette burn on thigh
(c) cut on lip
(d) bruises on forehead

70. Which of these is a member of the primary health care team?

(a) environmental health officer
(b) social worker
(c) district nurse
(d) dietician

71. Which group of people is frequently helped by CRUSE?

(a) dependants of sailors
(b) widows
(c) alcoholics
(d) drug addicts

72. A student hears a mother of a child in 'her' class say that she has a lot to do with gingerbread. She could assume from this that:

(a) she is trying to conquer a sweet tooth
(b) she does outside catering
(c) she is a single parent
(d) she works for a pop group fan club

73. Al-Anon is a support organisation for:

(a) alcoholics
(b) victims of motoring accidents
(c) relatives of alcoholics
(d) victims of crime

74. On joining the staff of a day nursery, a qualified nursery nurse is told by a colleague that their nursery Officer-in-Charge is very democratic. This means:

(a) she involves the whole staff in decision-making
(b) she has very strong political views
(c) she makes most decisions on her own
(d) she lets each member of staff make her own individual decisions

75. Good home/school links are vital if children are going to reap full benefit from their nursery/school experience. A head teacher hoping to establish such good links with 'new' families would be advised in the first instance to:

(a) call a meeting and give a short simple talk about the school
(b) create an 'open house' atmosphere and encourage parents in at any time
(c) send out a booklet containing all necessary information
(d) hold a jumble sale and get the parents involved and mixing

76. The head teacher of a nursery school expresses dissatisfaction with a student's wall display and asks her to take it down. The student should:

(a) ask for guidance for future display work
(b) politely refuse to do so
(c) explain firmly why she thinks it was acceptable
(d) put on a good face and comply

77. A trained nursery nurse working as nanny to a family is experiencing much fault-finding, and clashes of ideas on good child-rearing practice from her employer. She would be advised to:

(a) continue with the situation until her minimum agreed period of employment is reached
(b) ignore the tensions as far as possible and concentrate on the children, excluding the parents
(c) arrange time for a full discussion with her employers about sources of dissatisfaction
(d) argue out each incident with her employer, as it occurs

78. While at a local supermarket, a student is approached by a woman whose child is at the student's placement. The mother asks what it was that got her six-year-old son into trouble the week before. The student should:

(a) reassure the mother that it was nothing serious
(b) explain the incident tactfully and help her see how he was in the wrong
(c) pretend she knows nothing about it
(d) suggest she visits the school and talks to the class teacher

79. As a qualification on its own, in which sphere of work is the NNEB certificate most likely to offer career structure and promotion prospects to those who hold it?

(a) day nursery
(b) the private sector (nanny)
(c) special care baby unit
(d) infant school

80. A qualified nursery nurse is working for a family which appears to be breaking up. Her best immediate course of action is to:

(a) ask the parents tactfully about what is going to happen
(b) prepare the children through stories and discussion for the possible break-up
(c) maintain the children's established framework until informed of imminent changes
(d) give in her notice as she does not want to get involved

EXAMPLE 2 OF AN ESSAY PAPER

You will have three hours for the whole paper, and must answer one question from each of Sections A, B, C and D. The maximum marks for these are shown in the right hand column.

SECTION A

		Marks
A1	What are the causes of constipation in a child?	10
	How could you avoid this occurring?	10
	or	
A2	Describe the physical appearance and stage of development of a normal child aged six months.	12
	What progress can be expected in the next six months of life?	8

SECTION B

B1 Consider the following questions asked by a child of five years.

(a) Where do rain puddles go?
(b) Where did the guinea pig's babies come from?
(c) Why is the sea sometimes up here, and sometimes out there?

How would you answer TWO of these questions, providing factual information? 12

How might you develop further interest in ONE of these questions? 8

or

B2 Describe how you would organise painting activities in your nursery OR infant class. 10

Say how children benefit from these activities. 10

SECTION C

C1 'Our cultural background has a lasting influence upon us all.'
Discuss this statement, drawing upon your own experiences 20

or

C2 A mother of two children aged two and four has recently died of cancer, leaving the father to cope alone.
What problems might he encounter? 12
What sources of help are available? 8

SECTION D

D1 Most parents are not trained for their parental role.
Does a nursery nurse's training prepare her in any special way for the care and upbringing of children? 20

or

D2 After being unemployed for six months following your NNEB course, you are offered two jobs on the same day, one as a nursery nurse in a small maternity unit and the other in a children's hospital.
What are the main differences between the two jobs? 14
Which would you choose and why? 6

Here is one way in which a good candidate might answer Sections A, B, C and D.

SECTION A

Reasons for choice

I would choose to answer A2 in this section because I have been observing a baby called Sarah over the past three months. She is now seven months old and I have seen her every two weeks at home. I have compared her progress and development with a chart of normal 'milestones', so I know that she is an average baby doing all the things she should be doing. I find it much easier to write about a child I know because I can picture her in my mind, and this means more than just recalling notes.

I would not choose A1 if I could help it, because my knowledge of constipation in children is not extensive and I don't think I could write enough to justify all those marks.

A2: Plan of my answer

	6 months	*9 months*	*12 months*
APPEARANCE	Bright eyes, clear skin, healthy.	ditto	ditto
DISPOSITION	Happy, alert, interested; may be shy.	May be clingy to mother	
FOOD	Breast milk and solids.		Family meals, cow's milk.
LARGE MOVEMENTS	Sits with support. Turns from back to front.	Sits alone and crawls.	Stands. Walks with support. May walk alone.
SMALL MOVEMENTS	Can hold toy and look at it.	Pass from hand to hand.	
	Palmar grasp	Forefinger and thumb	
SPEECH	Crows, babbles	Vocalising	Vocalising; can say 8 words with meaning
TEETH	1–2	2–4	8
WEIGHT	7 kg	8.7 kg	10.0 kg
HEIGHT	65 cm	70 cm	73 cm

N.B. If you cannot remember heights and weights, just leave them out – they are not important.

Essay

Sarah is a healthy six-month-old girl. She has bright blue eyes, a snub nose and wispy blonde hair. Her skin is very clear and she has nice rosy cheeks. When she smiles (which is often) she reveals two tiny teeth in the front of her bottom jaw. Her body is rounded with firm, solid muscles. When she was last weighed she was 7.5 kg and her height was 65 cm.

Sarah has a happy, friendly disposition, and although sometimes shy initially when people stop and talk to her, she usually responds quickly to friendly chat with lots of babbling. She squeals with delight when you pretend to tickle her.

She loves going out in her pram. She sits up straight, supported by a cushion, and shows a great interest in her surroundings. Sarah needs safety straps on all the time she is in her pram because she is so active and could easily fall out.

When placed on the floor, Sarah likes to lie on her back and play with her toes, which she recently discovered. She can roll from back to front and manages to move towards a wanted toy by making 'swimming' movements along the floor. Also, whilst on her front, she can raise her head and shoulders very well by placing her hands flat on the floor doing 'press ups'. She can sit on the floor unsupported for a short time but then falls over, so her mother needs to put pillows around her to help keep her upright. When she is sitting like this, her favourite toy is a combined rattle/teething ring, which consists of triangular plastic shapes threaded on a chain. Sarah is able to hold this and look at it and can also put the plastic discs in her mouth. Usually everything you give her she puts into her mouth to taste and bite; this is partly to explore it, but also because she is teething, and biting makes her gums less painful. Watching her play on the floor, I notice that she picks up articles using her whole hand and has difficulty in letting go of the toys.

Sarah is breast-fed and now has three feeds a day, plus family meals. Her food is mashed rather than liquidised and she has just started to sit in her high chair to be spoon-fed by her mother. She has settled into a regular routine for meal-times and sleep. She always has a bath at night and really enjoys this as she can now splash and kick in the big bath – being supported by her mother, who usually gets very wet. She always cries when she comes out of the bath, but her mother soon soothes her, and after being dried and dressed she has a breast-feed and then sleeps from 7.0 p.m. to 7.0 a.m. During the day she will have a nap between 12.30 and 3.00 p.m. but for the rest of the day is alert and active.

In the next six months I would expect Sarah to make a tremendous amount of progress, especially in mobility and language development. By the age of one year she will have grown quite a bit as well. The average size of a one-year-old is height 73 cm and weight about 9.6 kg. She should also have cut some more teeth by then.

I would expect Sarah to be able to sit unsupported and to start crawling at nine months, so that by the age of one year she would have progressed to pulling herself to her feet and probably walking with the support of handy pieces of furniture. She may even be walking alone.

Her hands will become more adept and skilful at picking things up. From about eight months she will begin to use her thumb and index finger to pick up small objects and to pass toys from hand to hand, selecting and rejecting them. Using these skills, she will be attempting to feed herself, grabbing the spoon from her mother. 'Finger' food will be handled easily by the time she is a year old, although she may be diverted into using the food as play material if not hungry.

I would expect Sarah to have finished with breast-feeding at a year and to be drinking cow's milk from an ordinary cup with assistance from her mother.

Many children can say about eight words with meaning by the time they are a year old, but that does depend on the amount of stimulation they have had. Because Sarah's mum talks to her a lot and because she is very responsive, I am sure Sarah will be using some words and will certainly be able to make her needs known by the use of noises and gestures. At this stage of language development, the noises are vocalisations – that is, they sound like speech, having the same intonation, but when listened to carefully are only noises. At this stage also children understand much more than they can say and will obey (if they want to) simple instructions like 'Come to Mummy' and 'No, mustn't touch' etc.

Sarah may partly lose her friendliness between ten and twelve months and become shy and clingy to her mother, but this will be only a temporary phase and will soon be over. From being a 'mother's girl' at six months, by a year Sarah will have discovered that Dad is fun to be with too, and so is Granny and other familiar adults. She will begin to move away from dependence on her mother only and to include other people in her enlarging social circle. One-year-olds enjoy participating in games such as 'pat a cake' and 'round and round the garden'. They are able to anticipate what is coming when the game starts, and show all the signs of enjoyment. They also enjoy repetition.

I look forward to seeing Sarah grow up because it is fascinating to watch how a baby develops from a helpless being to an independent child in such a short time.

SECTION B

Reasons for choice

I would choose B2, the painting question, because it is an activity I take part in every day at placement. Also, I am quite a creative person and really enjoy seeing children's efforts develop.

I would avoid B1 as I think it would be difficult to explain clearly what I would tell a child.

B2: Plan of my answer

1. *Provision*: Siting, materials, protection, presentation, Adult interaction. Different art techniques. Aids to creativity. Things to avoid.

2. *Benefits*: Pleasure, avenue of expression, novelty, imagination, creativity, knowledge, emotional release, physical benefits, experimenting, introduction to beauty.

Essay

Painting materials act like a magnet to many nursery children, so the nursery nurse needs to play her full part in ensuring that they are provided in such a way that the children will not be disappointed.

Painting activities need a good light, and sufficient space and elbow room. Whether these activities are to take place on easels, on tables, or on the floor, these two facts must be borne in mind. Nothing is more frustrating than a horde of little – or big – feet trampling over a work of art, or a child being jogged or made to spill paint by his neighbour.

A variety of brushes, all fairly long-handled but differing in width, should be offered. Decorators' brushes can be effective, especially for covering large expanses quickly. These can also be pressed into service for use with clean water in a bucket outdoors for water painting on fences, walls, or the ground. Fine artists' brushes have no place with nursery children.

Paint must be of the correct consistency so that it neither runs down the paper exasperatingly when wet, nor causes the paper to buckle and crack when dry. The textbooks often recommend 'salad cream consistency', and this can be achieved by adding a little wall-paper paste.

Poster or powder paint is best. It is possible to mix up a week's supply and keep it in screw-top jars in a stock cupboard. Alternatively, it can be mixed daily with the help of the children. Primary colours and black and white are essentials. When possible, children should be permitted to mix their own shades of greys, browns and greens.

Non-spill pots, kept in a wooden rack or small milk crate, will eliminate waste and frustration. They are quite expensive to buy, and improvised ones can be made by cutting the top third off a washing-up liquid bottle and inserting it, inverted, in the base. One brush per pot should be the rule.

Paper of varied size, shape, texture and colour should be offered. It should always be cut – not torn. Although cheap, rectangular pieces of white kitchen paper are uninspiring, wallpaper samples from decorators' books can give interesting effects; so can unexpectedly-shaped pieces of old backing paper, put to good use a second time. Out-of-date travel posters can be begged from travel agents to provide large pieces for friezes and wall pictures. Paper should be securely anchored to easels with clips or clothes pegs.

The floor in a painting area may need protection; large polythene sheeting or newspaper will suffice. The children, too, will need to be protected; their overalls should be easy for them to cope with alone. Avoid thin 'ties' which will quickly become knotted and encrusted with paint. A corresponding number of overalls to painting places is a handy way of limiting the number of painters at any one time. Children readily accept this method.

The children should be trained to hang up their overalls after use and to wash their hands after painting. There must be adequate provision for paintings to dry.

All painting materials should be kept clean, bright and attractive-looking. An easel tray or board 'gunged up' with paint is not appealing; neither are six pots of khaki-coloured paint.

There is no substitute for free, undirected, spontaneous painting of the kind suggested here. But now and again, special 'techniques' with paint can be suggested. These are numerous, and afford the children excitement, novelty, some success and a sense of achievement.

Such techniques are usually carried out in a small group, and this means there will be much conversation and interaction with an adult. The children will be watching and concentrating, carrying out instructions, comparing and experimenting.

Finger-painting, with an extra thick mixture of paint and paste, on a suitable washable surface or piece of polythene sheet, enables a child to luxuriate in the sensory experience, and gain confidence in handling paint. This approach is particularly suitable for the younger children. Prints can be 'taken off' the resulting patterns. Slightly older or more experienced children can use cardboard 'combs' or forks to make paste patterns.

Blowing with a straw into a bowl filled with paint, water and washing-up liquid, and then holding a piece of paper over the top, is a very popular activity. The resulting prints can be attractively cut out, mounted and displayed.

Leaf printing is another technique which lends itself to attractive displays. Printing can also be carried out with a variety of household objects – interestingly shaped pieces of sponge foam, fruit and vegetables. Everyone knows about potato printing, but green peppers, oranges and wedges of white cabbage give more attractive results, and awaken children to pattern, shape and design.

'Blobbing' paint with a dropper or straw on to paper, and then blowing sideways at it through a straw produces seaweed-like effects. Alternatively, the blobs can be scattered on one side of the paper only and 'blotted' on the other – first ideas of symmetry here.

Marble-rolling in a shallow tray lined with paper – the marbles having been first dipped in thick paint – is a different approach, and one that demands co-ordination and control.

Wax-resist drawing, done with a candle and then washed over with thin paint, can seem like magic, but because results are a little delayed, this technique is more suited to the older, abler children.

An atmosphere that is conducive to children's creativity is essential. Some children like to talk about their painting, others do not want to be pressed to do so. Certainly, asking, 'What is it?' should be avoided – as should other attempts to superimpose adult standards and expectations on little children.

Creativity can be stifled by the adult doing large outlines for a wall picture and asking the children to fill them in. If a large figure outline is required, ask a child to lie down and then paint or draw round him. This approach is child-centred; it is also fun and gives rise to conversation about parts of the body, size and shape.

Discussing characteristics of proposed subjects for painting in a group project, for instance, animals after a visit to the zoo – and looking at pictures in books, can give children confidence and enthusiasm.

Children should be allowed to take their paintings home whenever possible. A child's efforts should never be torn up or thrown away in his presence, but the child should be allowed to paint over or destroy his own work if he chooses. In all her approaches to painting the adult must show that she attaches value to children's work, and she should encourage parents and other children to do the same.

Properly organised and presented, painting affords a highly pleasurable novelty and a new avenue of expression for most nursery children. Many mothers are unable or reluctant to risk large enough materials – especially if they live in a small home.

Painting kindles imagination, and it fosters the creative impulse. It stimulates language as children can be encouraged to name colours, shades, shapes and textures. It allows emotional release – for instance, when a child repeatedly paints a snake or some other object of which he is afraid. Painting also offers a chance to relive or prolong the happiness of recent experiences. It encourages control, co-ordination and precision. Painting and drawing are first steps towards reading and writing.

Through painting, a nursery nurse can encourage a child to experiment and learn about textures, colour mixing, shape, size and consistency. Painting fosters appreciation of beauty, and it can introduce a young child to other creative activities, and add to his whole enjoyment of life.

This specimen answer first appeared in *Nursery World*, the baby and child care magazine.

SECTION C

I would choose C2 as, although it is a very sad subject, it is an interesting one, and easier to tackle than C1, as there is more with which to get to grips.

C2: Plan

Problems – grief, strain, loss, exhaustion, practical worries
Children – confusion, unhappiness, regressive behaviour
Help – work or not? Caring facilities – nanny, child-minder, day nursery, neighbours, statutory and voluntary help.

Essay

Death of a loved one is always exceedingly painful. In this case the father, besides feeling immense loss and sadness, may also be worn out by the strain of knowing for some time that his wife was dying. He may have had the distressing experience of seeing her become increasingly weak, in pain, desolate at the prospect of leaving the children. He may be physically worn out by much hospital visiting, or trying to maintain a reasonably normal life for the children, as well as coping with a sick wife.

Although he has, in a sense, been waiting for it, her death will leave a large gap in his life. The finality of it now, and an end to hospital visiting, etc., will bring a sort of cruel relief. He may feel guilty about this reaction, and guilty, too, about occasions when he became irritable, or let the strain show; maybe did not do enough for his wife (he now feels) when she was alive. There will be times when he cannot grasp the reality of it, and others when he will experience anger at his fate. 'Why me? Why her? Why us?' may be his anguished cry.

These are all normal features of the grieving process, and he will have to work through them, as all bereaved people must do. He will not have much time for idle brooding, however, because decisions will have to be made quickly. Is he going to keep on his job (assuming he is in work and has been able to manage while his wife was still alive)? Or is he going to give up work and rely on welfare benefits, at least while the children are young, and one is under school age? He must consider that, besides the children's best interests, he also needs to look after his own physical and mental health. He may come to the conclusion that staying at home every day he will get more depressed and out of touch with other people, particularly men. Being in the house may reinforce the sense of loss, which may make him less of a loving and lively father to his children. He may never get back on the career ladder if he once comes off it. This, to many men, brings a sense of failure and loss of self-esteem.

As to the children, their emotional state will be something else he will have to contend with, in the short and long term. At present, they will be miserable, confused. A key person has gone from their lives; their father is upset, and no fun any more. The little one cannot verbally express his feelings and may even keep asking for his mother. The elder one can only inadequately express what he feels. Perhaps at an unconscious level they believe their mother has gone because they were not better behaved, or because she did not love them enough. They may feel that everything they have known as secure and reliable is about to be snatched away from them, including their father and their home. In their confused state, their behaviour may regress, possibly in terms of toilet training, eating, bedtime and sleeping patterns, willingness to be handled by other people. They may be tearful, or quarrel more than usual, or apparently stunned into an unnaturally passive state. On the other hand, they may appear relatively untouched by the event, which may upset their father more than ever.

If he chooses to go on working, the best possible source of help available is probably a resident, or daytime, nanny, if the father's earning capacity will allow. Although the children may resent this outsider at first, if she is good and sensitive, she will quite quickly establish a stabilising and loving relationship with them. She could take over all the daytime care of the younger child, and journeys to and from school with the older one. She can be there in the school holidays, and maybe sometimes child-mind in the evenings, so that the father can retain his friendships and hobbies, which are all important in times of stress.

Less expensive than a nanny are the services of a registered child-minder, who could possibly also look after the five-year-old at the end of his school day. Given a warm, loving person, this comfortable home setting can be a good second-best to remaining in his own home.

If his economic and personal situation is severe, the father may be able to obtain a place for the small child at a Social Services day nursery, in which case it could be a very long day, as the day nursery may be some distance away from home and/or work. This long day could be helpful to the father, but not necessarily good for the child, who will have to share 'his' nursery officer with maybe five or six other children, at a time when he most needs one-to-one tender loving care. He may be too tired to benefit much from his limited contact time with father.

On a short-term basis, depending on where he lives, the father may be able to obtain a home aid/help who will take over the running of a home and family in times of crisis. This could enable the two-year-old to remain at home, and others in the family to come home to comfortable, organised surroundings and good meals.

Neighbours, and friends or relatives who live nearby, could be a useful source of help at 'uncovered' times, school holidays, etc. In such a situation as this onlookers can be both supportive, and quick to criticise. Also, good intentions at the time of the funeral fade away when helping becomes tedious.

If he decides to give up work and live on state aid, the father may be entitled to unemployment benefit. He will be entitled to one-parent benefit and supplementary benefit. He may get rent and rate rebates, if applicable, free school meals and uniform for the children, and free prescriptions, spectacles, dental treatment, etc. for himself. If he carries on earning, he can claim tax allowance for a nanny or housekeeper.

The National Council for One Parent Families, Gingerbread and the Council for Voluntary Service are among the agencies through whom he may obtain advice, support and companionship.

SECTION D

Reasons for choice

I would answer the second question here, partly because I would like to work in a children's hospital, having had some experience during my practical work at college, but also because I am running out of time and could answer this one in the form of a chart which would be quicker.

D1 is an interesting question but although I feel that nursery nurse training is the ideal preparation for parenthood, I would not be able to say much more than that statement.

D2: Plan of my answer

Transport – shift work – pay – babies versus children – length of contract – type of work – co-workers – promotion. Sum up advantages and disadvantages.

Essay

I would very carefully study the job descriptions of the two kinds of hospital and would consult any of my friends who were working in hospital so that I could get some idea of what would suit me best.

Then I would make a list of various conditions of work and make a comparison:

	Maternity Unit	Children's Hospital
Hours of work	2 days off together each week Shift work 37½ hours	Sometimes 3 days off together Shift work 37½ hours
Rates of pay	Standard plus shift allowance	Standard plus shift allowance
Nearness to home and availability of public transport	Journey involves 2 buses or 1 bus plus ¾ mile walk Infrequent buses Cost £5.50 per week Too far to use bike	One bus only. Runs every 15 minutes Cost £2.50 per week Could use bike in summer
Type of work	Care of newborn babies. Shared with mother	Care of sick children 0–16 years Play for the 0–5 years
Job satisfaction	New-born babies are helpless and I would enjoy caring for them. Only short term contact because mothers stay in for such a short time.	Satisfaction of seeing children get well. Older children respond more. Patients may be in a long time or come back again. Could be depressing if children die.
Variety	Same work, but many different mothers and babies.	Different illnesses. This hospital has policy of nursery nurses working 6 months on each ward.
Co-workers	Small unit has only one other nursery nurse. Midwives Students	2 nursery nurses on each of 10 wards. Sick children's nurses State enrolled nurses
Promotion prospects	Nil	Nil
Comments from friends	'Useful experience' 'Worth doing for 1 year' 'Helpful if going on to do Special Care work'	'Useful experience' 'Helpful if you want to go on to do sick nursing' 'Many nursery nurses do this job for years'

Conclusion:

Maternity Unit	*For*: I like young babies.	*Against*: Difficulty of access. Expense of access. Short-term job. Could be lonely – only one other nursery nurse. I don't want to go on to further training.
Children's Hospital	*For*: Easy and cheap access. Working with several other nursery nurses; professional support. Could stay for years.	*Against*: May be upsetting to see children ill.

Decision: to take the job offered in the children's hospital.

MULTIPLE CHOICE PAPER, EXAMPLE 1: CORRECT ANSWERS

The answers are shown in a form which resembles the grid method used in the actual examination. In each case the *correct* answer is indicated by an underline.

1	a	**b**	c	d
2	a	**b**	c	d
3	a	b	**c**	d
4	a	**b**	c	d
5	a	b	**c**	d
6	a	b	**c**	d
7	a	**b**	c	d
8	a	b	**c**	d
9	**a**	b	c	d
10	**a**	b	c	d
11	a	**b**	c	d
12	a	**b**	c	d
13	**a**	b	c	d
14	a	b	**c**	d
15	a	**b**	c	d
16	a	**b**	c	d
17	a	b	c	**d**
18	a	b	**c**	d
19	a	b	**c**	d
20	**a**	b	c	d
21	a	b	**c**	d
22	a	**b**	c	d
23	a	**b**	c	d
24	a	**b**	c	d
25	**a**	b	c	d
26	**a**	b	c	d
27	**a**	b	c	d
28	a	b	c	**d**
29	a	b	**c**	d
30	a	b	c	**d**
31	a	b	**c**	d
32	a	b	**c**	d
33	**a**	b	c	d
34	**a**	b	c	d
35	a	**b**	c	d
36	a	b	c	**d**
37	a	b	**c**	d
38	a	b	c	**d**
39	a	b	**c**	d
40	a	b	c	**d**
41	a	b	c	**d**
42	a	b	c	**d**
43	a	b	c	**d**
44	a	b	c	**d**
45	**a**	b	c	d
46	a	b	c	**d**
47	a	b	**c**	d
48	a	**b**	c	d
49	a	**b**	c	d
50	a	b	c	**d**
51	a	b	c	**d**
52	a	b	c	**d**
53	a	b	**c**	d
54	a	**b**	c	d
55	**a**	b	c	d
56	a	b	**c**	d
57	a	b	c	**d**
58	**a**	b	c	d
59	a	b	**c**	d
60	a	b	**c**	d
61	a	b	c	**d**
62	a	b	c	**d**
63	a	b	c	**d**
64	**a**	b	c	d
65	a	b	**c**	d
66	a	b	c	**d**
67	a	**b**	c	d
68	**a**	b	c	d
69	a	b	c	**d**
70	**a**	b	c	d
71	a	**b**	c	d
72	a	b	c	**d**
73	a	b	**c**	d
74	a	b	**c**	d
75	a	b	c	**d**
76	**a**	b	c	d
77	a	b	c	**d**
78	a	b	c	**d**
79	a	**b**	c	d
80	a	b	**c**	d

MULTIPLE CHOICE PAPER, EXAMPLE 2: CORRECT ANSWERS

1	a	b	c	**d**
2	a	**b**	c	d
3	a	b	**c**	d
4	a	b	c	**d**
5	a	b	**c**	d
6	a	b	c	**d**
7	a	b	**c**	d
8	a	b	c	**d**
9	**a**	b	c	d
10	a	b	c	**d**
11	**a**	b	c	d
12	**a**	b	c	d
13	a	**b**	c	d
14	**a**	b	c	d
15	**a**	b	c	d
16	a	**b**	c	d
17	a	b	**c**	d
18	a	b	**c**	d
19	a	b	**c**	d
20	**a**	b	c	d
21	a	b	c	**d**
22	**a**	b	c	d
23	a	**b**	c	d
24	**a**	b	c	d
25	**a**	b	c	d
26	**a**	b	c	d
27	a	b	c	**d**
28	**a**	b	c	d
29	a	b	c	**d**
30	a	**b**	c	d
31	a	b	c	**d**
32	a	**b**	c	d
33	a	b	**c**	d
34	a	b	c	**d**
35	**a**	b	c	d
36	a	b	**c**	d
37	a	b	**c**	d
38	a	b	c	**d**
39	a	b	**c**	d
40	a	**b**	c	d
41	a	b	c	**d**
42	**a**	b	c	d
43	a	b	**c**	d
44	a	b	c	**d**
45	a	b	c	**d**
46	a	b	**c**	d
47	a	b	c	**d**
48	a	**b**	c	d
49	a	b	c	**d**
50	**a**	b	c	d
51	a	b	**c**	d
52	a	b	c	**d**
53	**a**	b	c	d
54	a	**b**	c	d
55	a	b	**c**	d
56	a	b	**c**	d
57	a	b	c	**d**
58	a	b	c	**d**
59	a	**b**	c	d
60	**a**	b	c	d
61	**a**	b	c	d
62	**a**	b	c	d
63	a	b	c	**d**
64	a	b	**c**	d
65	a	b	**c**	d
66	a	**b**	c	d
67	a	b	**c**	d
68	a	b	**c**	d
69	a	**b**	c	d
70	a	b	**c**	d
71	a	**b**	c	d
72	a	b	**c**	d
73	a	b	**c**	d
74	**a**	b	c	d
75	a	**b**	c	d
76	**a**	b	c	d
77	a	b	**c**	d
78	a	b	c	**d**
79	**a**	b	c	d
80	a	b	**c**	d